BEARS

By S.L. Hamilton

VISIT US AT
WWW.ABDOPUBLISHING.C

Published by ABDO Publishing Company, 8000 West 78th Street, Suite 310, Edina, MN 55439. Copyright ©2010 by Abdo Consulting Group, Inc. International copyrights reserved in all countries. No part of this book may be reproduced in any form without written permission from the publisher. A&D Xtreme™ is a trademark and logo of ABDO Publishing Company.

Printed in the United States of America, North Mankato, Minnesota.
102009
012010

Editor: John Hamilton
Graphic Design: Sue Hamilton
Cover Design: John Hamilton
Cover Photo: Getty Images
Interior Photos: AP-pgs 6, 7, 16, 17, 28, & 29; Corbis-pgs 1, 8, & 9;
Getty Images-pgs 2, 3, 4, 5, 7, 10, 11, 14, 15, 18, 19, 20, 21, & 32;
iStockphoto-pgs 10, 12, 13, 24, 25, 26, 27, 30, & 31;
Photo Researchers-pgs 22 & 23

Library of Congress Cataloging-in-Publication Data

Hamilton, S.L., 1959-
  Bears / S.L. Hamilton.
    p. cm. -- (Xtreme predators)
  Includes index.
  ISBN 978-1-60453-990-5
  1. Bears--Juvenile literature. 2. Bear attacks--Juvenile literature/
  I. Title.
  QL737.C27H359 2010
  599.78--dc22
                        2009035077

CONTENTS

XTREME

Bears are predators made to rule their world. Super-strong muscles with inches-long claws and teeth put them at the top of the food chain.

BEARS

CLAWS

Brown bears (including grizzly and kodiac bears) use their claws to dig for roots and to protect themselves.

& PAWS

Grizzly claws can be 3.5 inches (9 cm) long. Bears sharpen these lethal tools on trees.

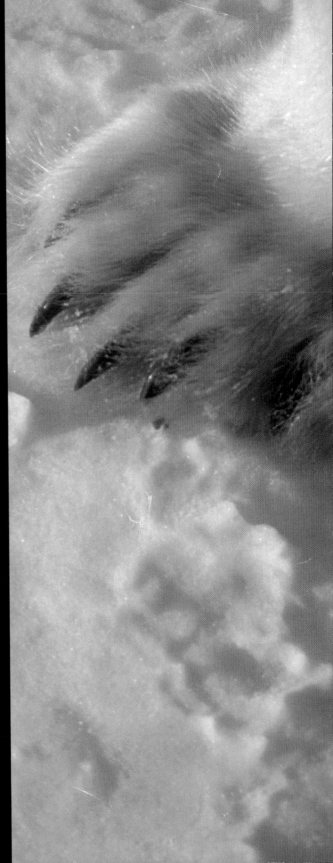

Polar Bear Claws

The largest of bears, the meat-eating polar bear has shorter claws than its forest-dwelling cousins. Polar bears' curved 2 inch (5 cm) claws are sharp. This provides traction on the ice for the big predators. The sharp claws also grip prey. Seals and walruses cannot wriggle free of a polar bear's mighty paws.

Xtreme Fact Bear claws are nonretractable. They are seen in a bear's track.

Sun Bear Claws

Sun bears of east Asia are the smallest species of bear. Only about 5 feet (1.5 m) in length, these rare, but aggressive bears get their name from the yellowish mark on their chests. Their claws are lightweight, but long and curved. These long nails make sun bears great tree climbers, and formidable foes.

In 1989, the San Diego Zoo's five new sun bears happily ripped up their home. Grass and trees were replaced with bear-proof items.

FANGS

Black bears have 42 teeth. In front are 4 pointy canines and 12 sharp incisors. Since black bears eat mostly plants, they also have 26 flat molars that grind their food into small pieces. In order to chew like this, black bears have developed strong jaw muscles. This also gives them a very hard bite.

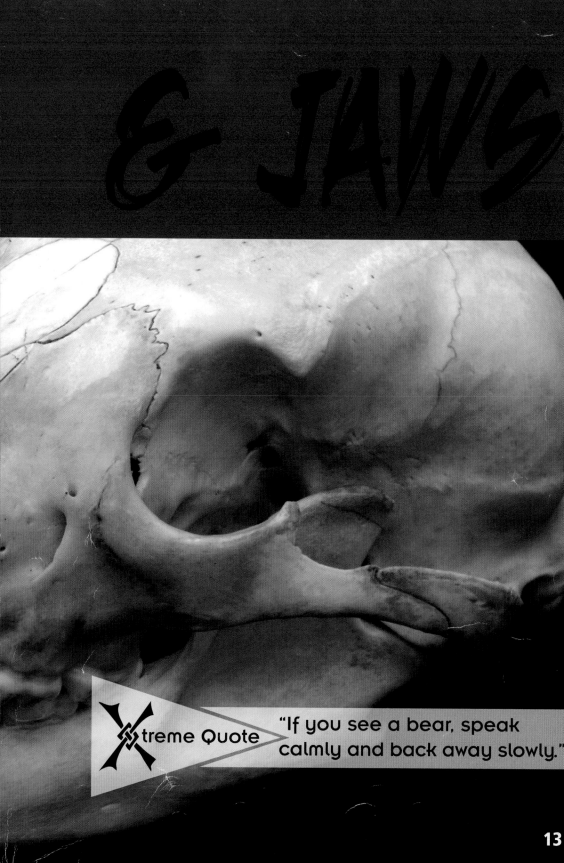

& JAWS

13

Grizzly Bears

Grizzly bears get their name from the gray tips of their fur. Like black bears, they are omnivores. Their teeth and jaws are strong enough to latch onto deer, caribou, and fish, but they also eat roots, berries, grass, and nuts.

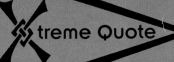

Xtreme Quote

"And she wasn't grabbing me with her paws, she was grabbing me with her teeth."
~Fran Nykoluk, grizzly attack survivor

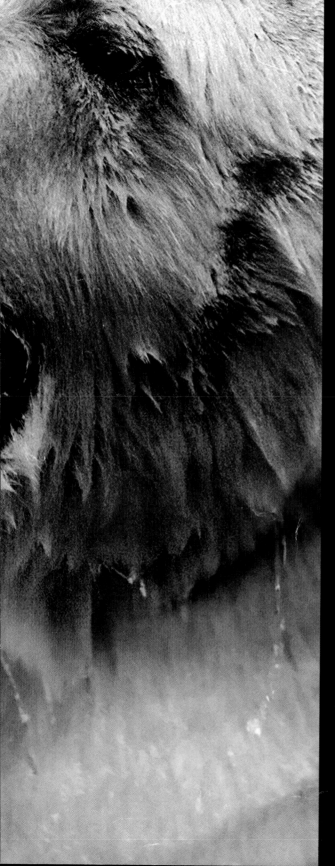

Polar Bears: Teeth for Meat

Polar bears have the same number of teeth as their plant-eating cousins, but their four canines are sharper, longer, and spaced farther apart. The extra-wide space allows this great predator to grab and tear at its meal without other teeth getting in the way.

SPEED

"It all happened so fast. Next thing I know, I'm just seeing teeth and trying to jump out of the way." ~Mark Matheny, Victim

DEMONS

Bear Speed: A Blur of Fur

Despite their bulk, bears are fast and agile. An average grizzly bear can run between 30 and 35 miles per hour (48 to 56 kph), much faster than an average human running less than 20 miles per hour (32 kph).

X **treme Fact** An average bear can run almost as fast as a horse.

THE BETTER TO

Polar bears see much
better than forest-dwelling bears.
With eyesight similar to humans, polar
bears also have a second eyelid over
each eye that may protect them from
snow blindness and help them
see underwater.

FIND YOU WITH

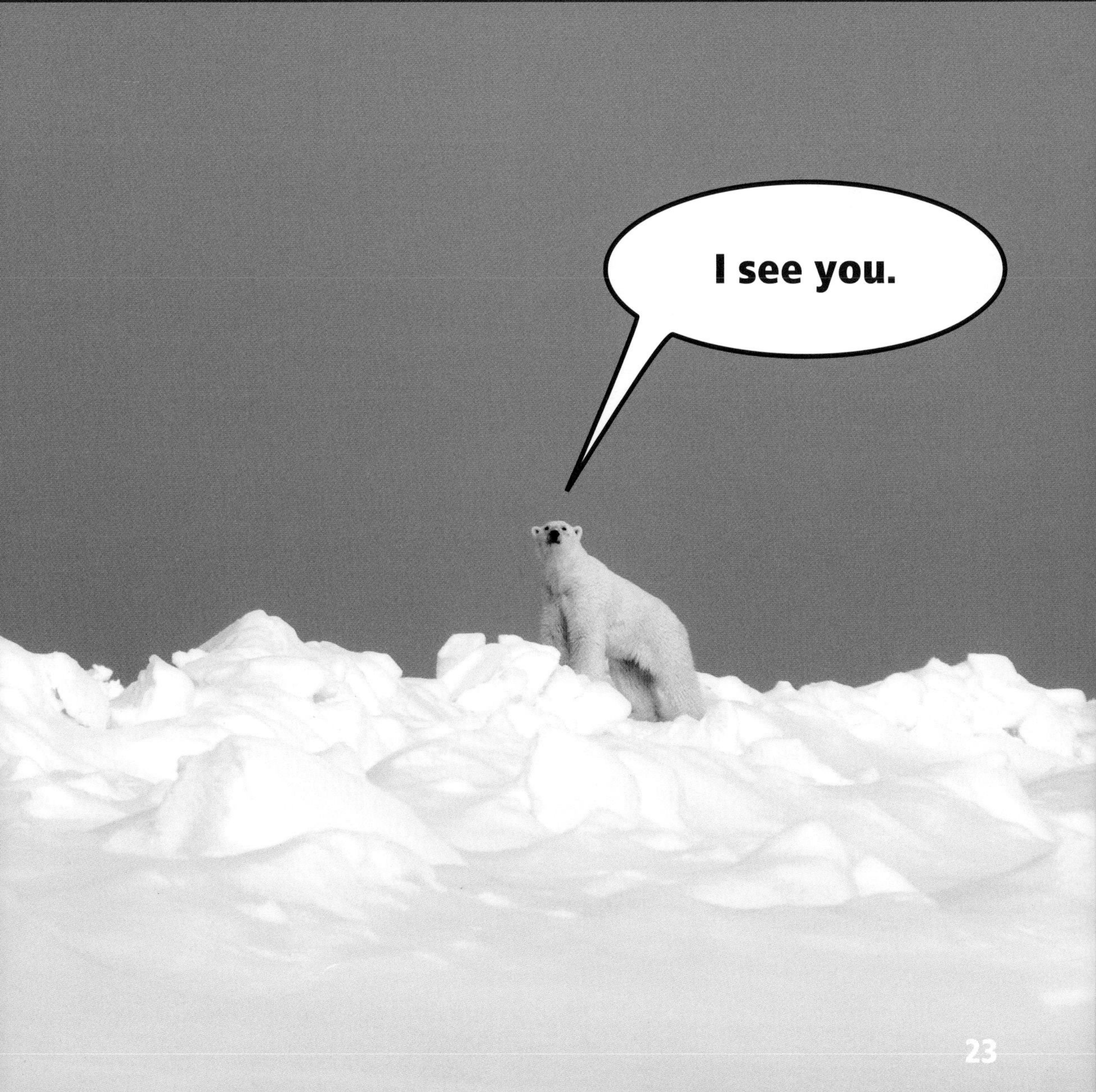

I Smell You

Bears may have the best sense of smell of any animal. Their noses are 2,100 times more sensitive than a human's sense of smell. Bears' noses help them find food, locate mates, keep track of cubs, and avoid danger. They know if there's a tube of toothpaste in a tent or a candy bar in a car.

Xtreme Fact

A bear can detect the smell of a dead animal from as far away as 20 miles (32 km).

Xtreme Fact

When a bear flattens down its ears, it is planning to attack.

I Hear You

Bears hear better than humans, probably in ranges similar to dogs. Bear ears vary in size and shape. Black bears have tall, pointed ears. Grizzlies have short, round ears. Polar bears have small ears to keep them from losing heat in the cold.

ATTACKS ON

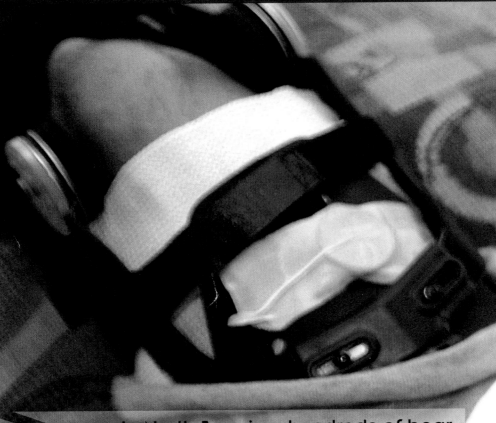

In North America, hundreds of bear encounters occur each year. But in the past century, less than 100 people have been killed.

Xtreme Fact

HUMANS

Bear attacks on humans are rare. They usually involve a mother bear protecting her cubs, or a bear that is surprised and feels threatened. When hiking in bear country, it is wise to stay in a group, make noise, and carry pepper spray.

Agile
Able to move fast.

Canine Teeth
Long, pointed teeth used for biting prey and ripping at meat. Also called fangs.

Food Chain
The process in nature where plants and animals are eaten by larger animals, and those animals are in turn eaten by even larger animals, and so on up the food chain. The largest, or most intelligent of creatures, are at the top of the food chain.

Incisors
Teeth found in the front of the mouth on both the top and bottom jaws. Used for cutting or gnawing.

Molars
Wide, flatter teeth used for grinding up food. Found in the back of the mouth.

GLOSSARY

Nonretractable Claws
Claws that cannot move back into a paw. Bears have nonretractable claws. Their claws are always out. Cats have retractable claws that move in and out of their paws.

Omnivore
Animals that eat both plants and meat.

Pepper Spray
A canned spray that burns and may sometimes cause temporary blindness, but does not kill.

Predator
An animal that preys on other animals.

Snow Blindness
Temporary blindness that is caused by eyes being exposed to extremely bright sunlight reflected off snow or ice.

INDEX